I0008055

WINDOWS PCs TROUBLESHOOTING FOR COMMON ISSUES USER GUIDE

How to Troubleshoot and Fix Windows 11, 10, and Earlier Versions of Windows System Issues

By

Delmar Benson

Contents

Introduction

The guide is designed to cover troubleshooting for **Windows 11** and **Windows 10**, as these are the most current and widely used versions of the Windows operating system. However, many of the basic and advanced troubleshooting techniques mentioned are also applicable to earlier versions like Windows 7 and 8. Specific features and tools unique to Windows 10 and 11, such as Windows Defender, the Windows Store, and the newer settings interface, are emphasized in the chapters.

Brief about Windows Operating Systems

When I think back on the evolution of Windows, it's incredible how far we've come. I've been working with various versions of Windows for years, and each iteration brings its own set of improvements, challenges, and quirks. If you're like me, you've probably seen firsthand how Windows has shaped the way we interact with computers, whether for work, entertainment, or everyday tasks.

Windows started its journey back in 1985 with a simple, graphical shell for MS-DOS, and since then, it has become the most dominant operating system in the world. Each new version has brought something innovative to the table. I remember when Windows 95 introduced the Start Menu- a feature that was revolutionary at the time and became the heart of the user experience. It was then that I truly felt the potential of personal computing expanding, making technology more accessible to everyone. As the years rolled on, Windows XP became a beloved staple, known for its stability and user-friendly interface. I spent countless hours navigating XP, appreciating its balance of functionality and simplicity. Windows 7 followed, polishing the user experience with Aero visuals and more robust performance.

To this day, many users still hold Windows 7 in high regard, and I completely understand why- it was dependable, efficient, and intuitive. Then came Windows 8, which, I have to admit, was a bit of a curveball. Microsoft aimed to bridge the gap between desktop and touch interfaces, but the radical changes left some users, including myself, a little bewildered. The Start Screen was a significant departure from the familiar Start Menu, and it took some getting used to. But as always with technology, it was a learning curve, and eventually, I found ways to navigate it effectively.

With the release of Windows 10, I felt like Microsoft had hit a sweet spot. It brought back the Start Menu, blending the best of both worlds from its predecessors. Windows 10 is versatile and capable of running on a wide range of devices, and it has a solid set of tools that make it easier to troubleshoot and maintain. I find that many of the improvements, such as the revamped Task Manager and virtual desktops, have made my workflow much smoother.

Now, with Windows 11, we're seeing yet another evolution. It's clear that Microsoft is focusing on a more modern, streamlined design, catering to a new era of computing where touch, voice, and pen input are becoming increasingly important. The updated interface is sleek, and I've noticed a shift towards productivity and creativity, with features like Snap Layouts and Widgets enhancing how we multitask and stay informed.

Each version of Windows has its strengths and weaknesses, but they all share a common goal: to provide a reliable and user-friendly environment for personal and professional computing. Throughout this book, I'll guide you through troubleshooting techniques that are applicable across these different versions, with a particular focus on Windows 10 and 11. Whether you're dealing with a stubborn software glitch or a hardware hiccup, understanding the operating system's evolution will give you a better grasp of how to solve the issues you encounter. After all, the more we know about where Windows has been, the better prepared we are to handle where it's going.

Understanding Windows Structure

When it comes to troubleshooting Windows, one of the first things I always emphasize is understanding the underlying structure of the operating system. Think of Windows as a well-organized library, where every book (or file) has its place, and every process has a role to play. Once you grasp how this structure is laid out, you'll find it much easier to navigate through the system and fix any issues that arise.

At the core of Windows is the file system, which is essentially the organizational scheme that Windows uses to store and retrieve data. Most of the time, we're working with the NTFS (New Technology File System) on modern Windows systems. NTFS is robust and includes features like file encryption, permissions, and the ability to handle large files and drives. This file system is what keeps everything in order, from the operating system files that make Windows run to the personal documents you create.

Navigating the file system starts with understanding the directory structure. When you open File Explorer, you'll notice a hierarchical layout that begins with the root directory, usually denoted as `C:\`. This root directory is the starting point for everything stored on your computer's main hard drive. From here, you'll see folders like `Program Files`, `Users`, and `Windows`- each serving a distinct purpose.

- **The `Windows` Folder**: This is the heart of the operating system. It contains all the essential files that Windows needs to run, including *system executables*, libraries, and configuration settings. If you're troubleshooting, it's important to be cautious when navigating this folder, as deleting or modifying files here can have serious consequences.

- **The `Program Files` and `Program Files (x86)` Folders**: These are where most of your installed applications live. The difference between the two lies in their architecture: `Program Files` is for 64-bit applications, while `Program Files (x86)` is for 32-bit applications. Understanding this distinction is crucial when you're troubleshooting application issues, as you may need to look in the right folder to find the application's files.
- **The `Users` Folder**: This is where you'll find all the user-specific data. Each user account on your computer has its own subfolder here, containing everything from documents and pictures to personalized settings. If you're troubleshooting issues related to a specific user profile—like missing documents or corrupted settings—this is the place to start.

Beyond the file system, another key aspect of Windows structure is its process management, which is handled by the Task Manager. I've found Task Manager to be one of the most powerful tools in the Windows toolkit. It gives you a real-time view of what's happening on your computer- everything from active applications to background processes, CPU and memory usage, and even network activity.

When you open Task Manager, the Processes tab is your go-to place for seeing what's running on your system. Here, you can identify which applications or services are using up your system resources and, if necessary, end tasks that are causing issues. The Performance tab, on the other hand, gives you a broader view of how your system is handling its workload, with detailed graphs showing CPU, memory, disk, and network usage. This is invaluable when you're diagnosing performance bottlenecks.

In addition to Task Manager, Windows comes with several built-in diagnostic tools that help you understand the system's inner workings. Tools like the Event Viewer, which logs system events and errors, and the Device Manager, which manages hardware components and drivers, are essential when you need to dig deeper into what's going wrong.

As you troubleshoot different issues, you'll find that understanding this basic structure- the file system, directory hierarchy, and process management- is like having a roadmap to the Windows operating system. Whether you're solving a minor inconvenience or tackling a more serious problem, knowing how Windows is organized will make the process smoother and more efficient. As you become more familiar with these elements, you'll start to see patterns and connections that make troubleshooting feel more intuitive.

General Troubleshooting Guidelines

Whenever I encounter a problem with a Windows PC, I like to approach it systematically. Over the years, I've developed a set of general troubleshooting guidelines that serve as my go-to strategies, no matter the issue. Following these steps can save you time and prevent the frustration that often comes with troubleshooting.

1. **Start with the Basics: Reboot Your System**

   It might sound cliché, but the first thing I do when something goes wrong is reboot the computer. A simple restart can clear out temporary glitches, reset hardware drivers, and reload system services. If your computer is running slowly, an application is unresponsive, or you're seeing odd behaviour, a reboot is often the quickest fix. It gives Windows a chance to start fresh and can resolve many issues without further intervention.

2. **Check for Windows Updates**

   Keeping your system up to date is crucial. Windows updates often include patches for security vulnerabilities, bug fixes, and improvements that can resolve existing problems. I always check for updates early in the troubleshooting process. To do this, go to **Settings > Update & Security > Windows Update** and click "Check for updates." If any updates are available, install them and restart your computer. Sometimes, installing the latest updates is all it takes to fix a stubborn issue.

3. **Use Built-In Troubleshooters**

Windows comes with several built-in troubleshooters designed to automatically detect and fix common problems. These tools can be a real time-saver. For example, if you're having trouble with your internet connection, there's a network troubleshooter that can help diagnose and resolve the issue. To access these troubleshooters, go to **Settings > Update & Security > Troubleshoot**. From there, you can select the appropriate troubleshooter based on the problem you're experiencing, such as audio playback, printer issues, or Windows Update failures.

4. **Perform a System Restore**

If you notice that your computer started acting up after installing new software or drivers, performing a System Restore can help. System Restore allows you to roll back your system to a previous state—before the issue began—without affecting your personal files. I find this particularly useful when a recent change has caused instability or performance problems. To use System Restore, type "Create a restore point" into the search bar, click on "System Restore," and follow the prompts to restore your system to an earlier date.

5. **Check for Hardware Issues**

Sometimes, what seems like a software problem is actually related to hardware. Loose cables, failing hard drives, or overheating components can all cause a range of issues. I always check the physical connections first—make sure everything is plugged in securely, and that your peripherals are functioning correctly. If you suspect a hardware issue, tools like the Windows Memory Diagnostic or third-party utilities like CrystalDiskInfo can help you identify failing hardware components.

6. **Review Recent Changes**

When a problem suddenly appears, I like to think back to any recent changes made to the system. Did you install a new program, update a driver, or connect a new device? These changes can sometimes introduce conflicts or bugs. If you suspect a specific change caused the problem, try reversing it—uninstall the software, roll back the driver, or disconnect the device—and see if that resolves the issue.

7. **Run a Virus and Malware Scan**

Malware can cause all sorts of strange behaviour on a Windows PC, from performance slowdowns to unexpected crashes. I make it a habit to run a full system scan with Windows Defender or a trusted third-party antivirus program if I suspect a security issue. Even if your antivirus hasn't flagged anything, it's worth running a deep scan to rule out the possibility of malware as the root cause of the problem.

8. **Check for Disk Errors**

Over time, your hard drive can develop errors that impact system performance and stability. Running a disk check can help identify and fix these issues. I use the built-in CHKDSK utility for this. To run it, open Command Prompt as an administrator, type `chkdsk /f`, and then press Enter. You'll need to restart your computer for the scan to run. If CHKDSK finds and repairs errors, it could resolve the problems you're experiencing.

9. **Review System Logs**

When standard troubleshooting doesn't provide answers, diving into system logs can offer more insights. I use the Event Viewer to review system logs and identify recurring errors or warnings. This tool logs events like application failures, system errors, and hardware issues, which can give you clues about what's going wrong. Access Event Viewer by typing "Event Viewer" into the search bar and navigating through the logs in the "Windows Logs" section.

10. **Know When to Seek Help**

Even with all these tools and strategies, some issues can be too complex to handle on your own. If you've tried everything and the problem persists, it might be time to seek professional help. Whether it's reaching out to a tech-savvy friend, contacting customer support, or visiting a repair shop, don't hesitate to ask for assistance when needed. Sometimes, a fresh perspective can make all the difference.

Chapter 2: Startup and Boot Issues

Common Boot Problems

One of the most unnerving moments for any PC user is when your computer refuses to boot properly. Over the years, I've encountered a variety of boot problems, and each one requires a different approach. Here's how I typically tackle the most common boot issues you might face with a Windows PC.

1. Black Screen of Death (BSOD)

The Black Screen of Death is one of the most frustrating boot issues because it often leaves you staring at a blank screen with no error message to guide you. When this happens, I usually start by checking the basics:

- **Monitor and Cable Connections**: Ensure that your monitor is turned on and properly connected to the computer. A loose or faulty HDMI or VGA cable can easily cause a black screen.
- **Check for External Devices**: Sometimes, external devices like USB drives, printers, or even external hard drives can interfere with the boot process. Disconnect all peripherals and try booting again.
- **Try Safe Mode**: If the black screen persists, booting into Safe Mode can help. To do this, restart your computer and press `F8` or `Shift` + `F8` repeatedly during startup to access the Advanced Boot Options. Safe Mode loads only the essential drivers and services, which can help you identify if a third-party driver or software is causing the issue.

2. Blue Screen of Death (BSOD)

Unlike the black screen, the Blue Screen of Death (BSOD) usually provides an error code or message, which can give you a clue about what's wrong. BSODs are often caused by hardware issues, driver problems, or critical system errors. Here's how I approach them:

- **Record the Error Code**: The error code on the blue screen (e.g., `0x0000007E`) is crucial for diagnosing the issue. I recommend taking a picture of the screen or writing down the code so you can research it later.
- **Use the Windows Troubleshooter**: If the system restarts after the BSOD, Windows will often attempt to diagnose the issue. I usually allow this process to complete, as it can sometimes fix the problem automatically.
- **Update Drivers**: Outdated or corrupt drivers are a common cause of BSODs. If you can boot into Safe Mode or access the system after a restart, I check Device Manager for any devices with a yellow exclamation mark and update or reinstall the drivers.
- **Check for Hardware Issues**: Faulty RAM or a failing hard drive can trigger BSODs. Running memory diagnostics or using tools like CHKDSK can help identify and fix these issues.

3. Slow Startup Times

When your computer takes forever to boot, it can be a sign of several underlying problems. Here's how I speed up a sluggish startup:

- **Disable Startup Programs**: Many applications are set to run at startup by default, which can significantly slow down the boot process. I use Task Manager to disable unnecessary startup programs. To do this, press `Ctrl + Shift + Esc` to open Task Manager, navigate to the **Startup** tab, and disable non-essential programs.
- **Check for Malware**: Malware can cause slow boot times by running malicious processes in the background. I always recommend running a full antivirus scan to rule out any infections.

- **Optimize System Resources**: Sometimes, the issue is that your computer is trying to do too much with limited resources. Upgrading your hardware, such as adding more RAM or switching to an SSD, can drastically improve boot times.

4. Stuck in a Reboot Loop

If your PC keeps restarting during the boot process, it's caught in a reboot loop. This can happen for a variety of reasons, from corrupt system files to hardware issues. Here's how I address it:

- **Boot into Safe Mode**: Again, Safe Mode is your best friend here. If you can access Safe Mode, you can troubleshoot further by running a System Restore, uninstalling recent updates, or repairing corrupted system files using the `sfc /scannow` command in Command Prompt.
- **Check for Recent Changes**: If the problem started after a recent driver update or software installation, try rolling back the driver or uninstalling the software.
- **Repair Startup**: If the reboot loop persists, I use the Windows Recovery Environment to perform a Startup Repair. You can access this by booting from a Windows installation media (USB or DVD) and selecting **Repair your computer > Troubleshoot > Advanced options > Startup Repair**.
- **Run CHKDSK**: Corrupt disk sectors can also cause reboot loops. Running `chkdsk /r` from Command Prompt in the Recovery Environment can repair bad sectors and help resolve the issue.

5. No Bootable Device Found

This error message usually indicates that your computer can't find a drive to boot from. Here's what I do to fix it:

- **Check BIOS/UEFI Settings**: Sometimes, the boot order in the BIOS or UEFI settings gets changed, causing the system to look for a bootable device in the wrong place. I enter the BIOS/UEFI by pressing `Del`, `F2`, or another key specific to the manufacturer during startup and ensure that the primary hard drive is set as the first boot device.

- **Check the Hard Drive Connection**: A loose or disconnected hard drive can also cause this error. I open the computer case (if comfortable) and check the hard drive cables to ensure they're securely connected.
- **Repair the Boot Sector**: If the boot sector is corrupted, Windows won't boot. I use the Windows Recovery Environment to repair the boot sector by running commands like `bootrec /fixmbr`, `bootrec /fixboot`, and `bootrec /rebuildbcd` in the Command Prompt.

6. Missing Operating System

Seeing a "Missing Operating System" message can be alarming, but it doesn't always mean your data is lost. Here's how I address this:

- **Check BIOS/UEFI Boot Order**: Just like with the "No Bootable Device Found" error, I start by checking the boot order in the BIOS/UEFI settings to ensure the correct drive is selected.
- **Repair the Master Boot Record (MBR)**: A corrupted MBR can prevent Windows from recognizing the operating system. I use the same `bootrec` commands mentioned above to repair the MBR.
- **Restore from Backup**: If the operating system is truly missing or corrupted beyond repair, I may need to restore from a backup or reinstall Windows. It's always a good reminder to regularly back up your data to avoid complete data loss in such scenarios.

Improving System Speed

Over time, every Windows PC can start to feel sluggish, even if it was blazing fast when you first got it. I've had my fair share of slow systems, and it can be frustrating when simple tasks take forever to complete. But with the right approach, you can significantly improve your system's speed and get it running like new again. Here's how I usually tackle the issue:

1. Manage Startup Programs

One of the most common reasons for a slow system is too many programs launching at startup. These programs consume resources right from the get-go, which can significantly slow down your boot time and overall system performance.

- **Use Task Manager**: I start by opening Task Manager (press `Ctrl + Shift + Esc`) and navigating to the **Startup** tab. Here, you'll see a list of all the programs that start when Windows boots up. I look for programs I don't need to run automatically—like chat apps, update managers, or media players—and disable them. This won't uninstall the programs; it just stops them from running automatically at startup.

2. Uninstall Unnecessary Software

Over time, you might install programs that you no longer use, and these can clutter your system and use up valuable resources. Regularly cleaning up unnecessary software can free up disk space and improve performance.

- **Go to Settings > Apps > Apps & Features**: I review the list of installed programs and uninstall anything I don't use anymore. Be cautious not to remove anything critical to the system's operation—stick to programs you recognize and don't need.

3. Optimize Your Hard Drive

Your hard drive plays a significant role in how fast your system operates. Regularly optimizing your hard drive can help improve speed.

- **Defragment and Optimize Drives**: On traditional hard drives (HDDs), fragmentation can cause files to be spread out across the disk, making it take longer to read and write data. I use the built-in Defragment and Optimize Drives tool (type "defragment" into the search bar) to defragment my drives regularly. If you have a Solid State Drive (SSD), defragmentation isn't necessary, but the tool will still optimize the drive by running a trim command.
- **Consider Upgrading to an SSD**: If you're still using an HDD, upgrading to an SSD can be one of the most significant improvements you can make. SSDs are much faster than traditional hard drives, leading to quicker boot times, faster file access, and generally more responsive performance.

4. Clean Up Your Disk

Another factor that can slow down your system is a cluttered hard drive. Regularly cleaning up unnecessary files can help maintain speed.

- **Use Disk Cleanup**: Windows includes a Disk Cleanup utility that can help you remove temporary files, system cache, and other unnecessary data. I run Disk Cleanup (type "disk cleanup" into the search bar) and select the files I want to delete. Be sure to check the "System files" option to clean up even more space by removing outdated Windows update files or old installation files.

- **Empty the Recycle Bin**: I make it a habit to empty the Recycle Bin regularly, especially after deleting large files, to free up space.

5. Adjust Visual Effects

Windows includes various visual effects that make the interface look nicer but can also slow down performance, especially on older or less powerful machines.

- **Adjust for Best Performance**: I right-click on **This PC** and select **Properties** > **Advanced system settings** > **Settings** under Performance. From here, I choose "Adjust for best performance" to disable all visual effects or customize which ones to keep. This can make the interface look more basic, but it can also noticeably speed up your system.

6. Update Drivers and Software

Outdated drivers and software can cause performance issues, including system slowdowns.

- **Use Windows Update**: I make sure all system drivers are up to date by checking for updates under **Settings** > **Update & Security** > **Windows Update**.
- **Manually Update Drivers**: Sometimes, specific drivers—like those for your graphics card—require manual updates from the manufacturer's website. I check for the latest versions and update them as needed.
- **Keep Software Updated**: Outdated software can slow down your system or cause compatibility issues. I regularly update the programs I use, either through built-in update features or by downloading the latest versions from the developer's website.

7. Increase RAM

If your system is still slow after trying the above steps, it might be running low on memory (RAM). Upgrading or adding more RAM can help if you regularly run out of memory when using multiple applications or working with large files.

- **Check Current RAM Usage**: I monitor my system's RAM usage using Task Manager. If my RAM is frequently maxed out, it's a sign that an upgrade could help.
- **Upgrade RAM**: Adding more RAM is relatively straightforward for most desktops and some laptops. I check my system's specifications to see how much RAM it can support and consider upgrading if I'm running less than the recommended amount for my typical workload.

8. Disable Background Apps

Many apps continue to run in the background even when you're not using them, consuming resources and slowing down your system.

- **Manage Background Apps**: I go to **Settings > Privacy > Background apps** and disable background activity for apps that I don't need running all the time. This can free up system resources and improve performance.

9. Run a Virus and Malware Scan

Malware is a common cause of slow system performance. It can run in the background, consuming resources and causing various issues.

- **Use Windows Defender**: I run a full scan using Windows Defender (or another trusted antivirus program) to check for malware. Even if the scan doesn't find anything, it's good practice to ensure your system is clean.

- **Consider Third-Party Tools**: If you suspect your system is infected, tools like Malwarebytes can offer an additional layer of protection and detect threats that might slip past your primary antivirus software.

10. Use a System Optimization Tool

There are several reputable system optimization tools that can automate the process of cleaning up your system, managing startup programs, and even defragmenting your hard drive.

- **Choose a Trusted Tool**: I recommend using well-known tools like CCleaner or Advanced SystemCare. These tools can help you quickly identify and resolve performance issues, though it's important to use them carefully and avoid overly aggressive settings that might cause more harm than good.

Dealing with Resource-Hogging Applications

It's not uncommon for certain applications to start consuming more resources than they should, causing your system to slow down or become unresponsive. Over the years, I've encountered plenty of resource-hogging programs, and I've learned that identifying and managing them can make a big difference in your system's performance. Here's how I typically deal with these greedy applications.

1. Identify the Resource Hogs

The first step is to figure out which applications are using up the most resources. I always start with Task Manager, which gives a clear overview of what's happening on your system.

- **Open Task Manager**: I press `Ctrl + Shift + Esc` to open Task Manager and then click on the **Processes** tab. Here, I sort by **CPU**, **Memory**, or **Disk** to see which processes are consuming the most resources.
- **Look for Outliers**: I pay attention to any process using a disproportionate amount of CPU, memory, or disk space. If a particular application is consistently at the top, it's likely the culprit.

2. Close Unnecessary Applications

Once I've identified the resource hogs, the next step is to decide whether I really need those applications running. Often, the simplest solution is to close programs that aren't necessary.

- **End Task**: In Task Manager, I right-click on the offending process and select **End task**. This will immediately close the application and free up resources. However, I'm careful with this—closing certain system processes or unsaved work can cause data loss or instability.
- **Save Work First**: Before ending a task, I always make sure to save any work I have open in the application to avoid losing important data.

3. Investigate the Cause

Sometimes, an application using too many resources could be a sign of a deeper issue, such as a memory leak, poor optimization, or even malware.

- **Check for Updates**: I check if there's an update available for the application. Developers often release patches to fix bugs and improve performance.
- **Scan for Malware**: Resource-hogging behaviour can also be a sign of malware or a virus. I run a full antivirus scan using

Windows Defender or another trusted antivirus tool to rule out any malicious activity.

- **Review Recent Changes**: If the issue started after a recent update or software installation, I consider rolling back the update or uninstalling the new software to see if that resolves the problem.

4. Adjust Application Settings

Some applications allow you to adjust their settings to use fewer resources. This is particularly true for games, video editing software, or any other resource-intensive program.

- **Lower Graphics or Performance Settings**: In resource-intensive applications like games or video editing software, I lower the graphics settings or limit the number of simultaneous tasks. This can significantly reduce CPU and GPU usage.
- **Limit Background Processes**: I also check for any background processes the application might be running, such as auto-updates or indexing, and disable or limit them if they're not necessary.

5. Use Lightweight Alternatives

If an application consistently uses more resources than you'd like, it might be worth considering a lightweight alternative.

- **Explore Other Options**: For example, if you find that your web browser is using too much memory, consider trying a different browser known for being more resource-efficient. Similarly, if your media player or image editor is hogging resources, there are often less demanding alternatives available.

6. Limit Startup Programs

Some resource-hogging applications may start automatically when you boot up your PC, even if you don't need them right away.

- **Disable Unnecessary Startup Programs**: I go to Task Manager's **Startup** tab and disable any applications that I don't need to run as soon as my computer starts. This not only frees up resources but also speeds up boot time.

7. Check for Software Conflicts

Occasionally, multiple applications running simultaneously can conflict with each other, causing them to use more resources than usual.

- **Run Applications Separately**: If I suspect a software conflict, I try running the applications one at a time to see if the issue persists. If one application works fine alone but causes problems when another is running, it's likely a conflict.
- **Update or Reinstall**: I check for updates for the conflicting applications or consider reinstalling them to see if that resolves the issue.

8. Monitor System Performance

After addressing the resource-hogging applications, I continue to monitor my system's performance to ensure that the problem doesn't return.

- **Use Resource Monitors**: In addition to Task Manager, I sometimes use more advanced tools like the **Resource Monitor** (built into Windows) or third-party applications like **Process Explorer** to keep an eye on system resources.
- **Set Alerts**: Some monitoring tools allow you to set alerts when a certain resource threshold is exceeded. This can help

catch resource hogs early before they cause significant performance issues.

Upgrading Hardware vs. Software Solutions

When dealing with performance issues on a Windows PC, the decision often boils down to whether you should upgrade your hardware or stick to software solutions. I've faced this dilemma many times and have learned that the right choice depends on the specific problems you're encountering and the goals you have for your system. Let me break down the considerations that guide my decision-making process.

1. Assessing the Problem

Before deciding on an upgrade or a software solution, I first take the time to thoroughly assess the problem. Not every issue requires a hardware upgrade; sometimes, a few software tweaks can make a significant difference.

- **Identify Performance Bottlenecks**: I start by identifying where the bottleneck is occurring. Is the system slow to boot? Are applications taking a long time to load? Is there frequent freezing or crashing? Using tools like Task Manager or Resource Monitor helps me pinpoint whether the problem is related to the CPU, memory, disk usage, or something else.
- **Determine System Age**: If the PC is relatively new, software solutions might be more effective. However, if the hardware is outdated, it might not be able to keep up with modern software demands, indicating that an upgrade could be necessary.

2. Advantages of Software Solutions

Software solutions are often the first line of defence when dealing with performance issues. They're typically less expensive than hardware upgrades and can often resolve the problem without the need for new components.

- **Cost-Effective**: Software fixes, like cleaning up the disk, disabling startup programs, or adjusting system settings, are usually free or low-cost. For example, using built-in tools like Disk Cleanup or Task Manager can help improve performance without spending a dime.
- **Quick Implementation**: Implementing software solutions is generally quicker than a hardware upgrade. Tweaks like updating drivers, uninstalling unnecessary programs, or optimizing settings can be done in a matter of minutes or hours.
- **Non-Invasive**: Software solutions don't require opening up your PC, making them a less risky option, especially if you're not comfortable with hardware changes. These solutions often involve making changes within the operating system or applications, which is more straightforward for most users.

3. When Software Solutions Fall Short

While software solutions can address many issues, there are times when they might not be enough. If you've tried all the usual software fixes and your system is still struggling, it could be a sign that the hardware is the limiting factor.

- **Persistent Slowness**: If your PC remains sluggish even after optimizing settings, cleaning up files, and disabling unnecessary programs, the hardware might be too outdated to handle modern tasks effectively.
- **Inadequate Resources**: A common scenario is running out of RAM while multitasking. No amount of software optimization will make up for insufficient memory when trying to run resource-intensive applications. Similarly, if

your hard drive is nearly full or your CPU is consistently maxed out, software solutions might only offer temporary relief.

4. Advantages of Hardware Upgrades

When software solutions aren't enough, upgrading your hardware can provide a significant and long-lasting boost in performance. I've found that the most impactful hardware upgrades usually involve increasing memory (RAM), upgrading storage to an SSD, or upgrading the CPU or GPU.

- **Dramatic Performance Gains**: A hardware upgrade, such as adding more RAM or switching from an HDD to an SSD, can drastically improve your system's speed and responsiveness. For instance, upgrading to an SSD can cut boot times in half and make file operations much faster.
- **Extended System Life**: Upgrading hardware can extend the life of your system, delaying the need to purchase an entirely new PC. This is particularly useful if your PC is still in good condition but just needs a bit more power to keep up with current demands.
- **Better Handling of Modern Software**: As software becomes more demanding, older hardware might struggle to keep up. Upgrading components like the CPU or GPU allows your system to handle modern applications and games more efficiently.

5. When to Consider Hardware Upgrades

There are specific scenarios where a hardware upgrade is clearly the best choice. Here's when I typically opt for new components:

- **Severe Performance Bottlenecks**: If Task Manager consistently shows that your CPU, memory, or disk is maxed out, and software solutions haven't helped, it's time to consider an upgrade.

- **Running Modern Applications**: If you're trying to run newer, more demanding applications (like video editing software or modern games) on an older system, upgrading the hardware might be necessary to achieve acceptable performance.
- **Frequent Hardware-Related Issues**: If you're experiencing frequent crashes, freezes, or blue screens, these could be signs that your hardware is failing or not up to the task. In these cases, replacing or upgrading the affected components can restore stability and performance.

6. Balancing Cost and Performance

When deciding between hardware and software solutions, cost is always a factor. Hardware upgrades can be expensive, so I weigh the potential benefits against the cost.

- **Cost-Benefit Analysis**: I ask myself whether the performance gains from a hardware upgrade justify the expense. For example, upgrading to an SSD is relatively affordable and can provide a significant boost in speed, making it a worthwhile investment. On the other hand, upgrading the CPU or GPU can be costly, so I consider whether it's better to save that money toward a new system in the future.

Consider Future Needs: I also think about how long I plan to keep the system. If I'm expecting to use it for several more years, investing in hardware upgrades makes sense. But if I'm planning to replace the system soon, I might stick with software solutions to hold me over until the upgrade.

Connectivity Issues

Few things are as frustrating as losing your internet connection in the middle of an important task. Over the years, I've dealt with my fair share of connectivity issues, and I've learned that while they can be annoying, they're usually fixable with the right approach. Here's how I tackle common connectivity problems on a Windows PC.

1. Identifying the Problem

The first step in resolving connectivity issues is identifying whether the problem lies with your PC, the router, or your internet service provider (ISP).

- **Check Other Devices**: I start by checking if other devices on the same network are also experiencing connectivity issues. If they are, the problem is likely with the router or the ISP. If only my PC is affected, it's probably a problem with the PC itself.
- **Test the Connection**: I try to connect to different websites to see if the issue is with a particular site or with the internet connection in general. If all sites are inaccessible, it's likely a broader connectivity issue.

2. Basic Troubleshooting Steps

Before diving into more complex solutions, I always start with these basic troubleshooting steps. Often, these simple actions can resolve the issue quickly.

- **Restart the PC and Router**: The first thing I do is restart both my PC and my router. This can reset the network connection and resolve many temporary issues. I turn off the router, wait for about 30 seconds, and then turn it back on. I also restart my PC to refresh its connection.

- **Check Network Cables**: If I'm using a wired connection, I make sure all cables are securely plugged in. I've found that loose or damaged cables can often be the culprit behind connectivity issues.
- **Toggle Wi-Fi**: For wireless connections, I toggle the Wi-Fi on and off to see if it re-establishes the connection. Sometimes, simply reconnecting to the network can fix the issue.

3. Network Adapter Troubleshooting

If basic troubleshooting doesn't resolve the issue, I move on to checking the network adapter, which is responsible for connecting your PC to the network.

- **Check the Network Adapter Status**: I open **Device Manager** (by typing "Device Manager" into the search bar) and expand the **Network Adapters** section. I look for any yellow exclamation marks or red Xs, which indicate a problem with the adapter.
- **Update Network Adapter Drivers**: Outdated or corrupted drivers can cause connectivity issues. I right-click on the network adapter and select **Update driver**. I then choose **Search automatically for updated driver software** to let Windows find and install the latest driver.
- **Disable and Re-enable the Adapter**: If the adapter appears to be functioning but the connection isn't working, I try disabling and then re-enabling it. Right-clicking on the adapter in Device Manager, selecting **Disable**, waiting a few seconds, and then selecting **Enable** can sometimes resolve the issue.

4. Network Reset

Sometimes, a more comprehensive reset of the network settings is necessary, especially if the issue persists despite the above steps.

- **Use Windows Network Troubleshooter**: Windows includes a built-in network troubleshooter that can automatically detect and fix common connectivity problems. I go to **Settings > Network & Internet > Status** and click on **Network troubleshooter**. I follow the prompts to diagnose and resolve any issues.
- **Network Reset**: If the troubleshooter doesn't help, I perform a network reset. This will reinstall network adapters and reset network settings to their defaults. I go to **Settings > Network & Internet > Status**, scroll down, and click **Network reset**. After the reset, I'll need to reconnect to Wi-Fi networks and reconfigure any VPNs or other network settings.

5. Checking for Interference

Wireless networks are susceptible to interference from other devices, which can cause connectivity issues, especially in crowded areas.

- **Change Wi-Fi Channels**: I log into my router's settings and change the Wi-Fi channel. Most routers are set to auto-select channels, but sometimes manually choosing a less crowded channel can improve connectivity. I look for channels with the least interference from neighbouring networks.
- **Relocate the Router**: If possible, I move the router to a central location in the house or office, away from walls and other obstructions. I also ensure it's not near devices like microwaves or cordless phones, which can interfere with the signal.

6. Advanced Troubleshooting

If the problem persists, I move on to more advanced troubleshooting techniques that delve deeper into the network settings.

- **Flush DNS Cache**: Corrupt or outdated DNS settings can cause connectivity issues. I open Command Prompt as an administrator and type `ipconfig /flushdns` to clear the DNS cache, followed by `ipconfig /release` and `ipconfig /renew` to refresh the IP address.
- **Manually Configure DNS Settings**: Sometimes, manually configuring DNS settings can improve connectivity. I go to **Control Panel > Network and Sharing Center > Change adapter settings**, right-click on my active network connection, and select **Properties**. Under **Internet Protocol Version 4 (TCP/IPv4)**, I select **Use the following DNS server addresses** and enter a reliable DNS server, such as Google's (8.8.8.8 and 8.8.4.4).
- **Check Firewall and Security Software**: Overly aggressive firewall or security software settings can block internet access. I check the settings to ensure they aren't preventing connectivity. Temporarily disabling the firewall or security software can help determine if it's the cause.

7. ISP and Router Issues

If all else fails, the issue may lie with your ISP or router, rather than your PC.

- **Contact ISP**: I contact my ISP to check if there are any known outages or issues in my area. Sometimes, they can provide additional troubleshooting steps or send a technician if the problem is on their end.
- **Update Router Firmware**: If the router is outdated or experiencing issues, updating the firmware can sometimes resolve connectivity problems. I log into the router's settings and check for firmware updates, which are usually found under the **Maintenance** or **Advanced** sections.

- **Consider a New Router**: If the router is old or consistently causes issues, it might be time to upgrade to a newer model with better performance and coverage.

Common Application Problems

Dealing with application issues can be one of the most frustrating aspects of using a Windows PC. Whether it's a program that won't start, crashes unexpectedly, or simply doesn't perform as it should, these problems can disrupt your workflow and cause a lot of headaches. Over the years, I've encountered many common application problems and developed a series of steps to troubleshoot and resolve them effectively.

1. Application Won't Start

When an application refuses to start, it can be due to a variety of reasons ranging from corrupted files to compatibility issues. Here's how I typically approach this problem:

- **Check for Error Messages**: First, I pay attention to any error messages that pop up when I try to launch the application. These messages can provide valuable clues about what's going wrong. For example, if the message mentions missing files or permissions, that's a good starting point for troubleshooting.
- **Run as Administrator**: Sometimes, applications require elevated privileges to run properly. I right-click on the application icon and select **Run as administrator** to see if that resolves the issue.
- **Check Compatibility Mode**: If I'm trying to run an older application on a newer version of Windows, compatibility mode can help. I right-click on the application, go to **Properties > Compatibility**, and select a previous version of Windows from the drop-down menu. This can often resolve issues with older software.

- **Reinstall the Application**: If the application still won't start, I consider reinstalling it. I go to **Settings** > **Apps** > **Apps & features**, find the application, and select **Uninstall**. After that, I download the latest version of the application from the official website and install it again.

2. Application Crashes or Freezes

An application that crashes or freezes frequently can be incredibly frustrating, especially if it happens during important tasks. Here's how I handle these issues:

- **Update the Application**: I start by checking if there's an update available for the application. Developers often release updates to fix bugs and improve stability. I look for an update option within the application itself or visit the official website to download the latest version.
- **Check for Conflicts**: Sometimes, other running applications or background processes can conflict with the one that's crashing. I try closing unnecessary programs to see if that resolves the issue. Additionally, I check Task Manager for any resource-hogging processes that might be interfering with the application.
- **Clear Application Cache and Data**: Some applications store temporary files or cache data that can become corrupted over time, leading to crashes. If the application has an option to clear cache or data, I use it. Otherwise, I might need to manually delete cache files located in the application's directory.
- **Run in Safe Mode**: If the application still crashes, I try running Windows in Safe Mode. Safe Mode loads only the essential drivers and services, which can help determine if the issue is caused by a third-party program or service. I restart the PC, press F8 or Shift+Restart, and select **Safe Mode**. If the application works in Safe Mode, it's likely that another program or service is causing the problem.

3. Application Running Slowly

When an application runs slowly or becomes unresponsive, it's often due to insufficient system resources or heavy background activity. Here's how I address performance issues:

- **Check System Requirements**: I start by checking if the application's system requirements exceed my PC's capabilities. This includes looking at CPU, RAM, and disk space requirements. If my system doesn't meet the minimum requirements, the application will naturally run slowly, and a hardware upgrade might be necessary.
- **Update Drivers**: Outdated or incompatible drivers can cause performance issues. I make sure that all drivers, especially for the graphics card and network adapter, are up to date. I visit the manufacturer's website or use Device Manager to update them.
- **Limit Background Processes**: I open Task Manager to see what else is running in the background. If there are unnecessary processes consuming a lot of CPU or memory, I close them to free up resources for the application.
- **Adjust Application Settings**: Many applications, especially those involving graphics or video processing, have settings that can be adjusted to improve performance. I look for options to reduce graphics quality, limit background tasks, or adjust resource usage within the application.

4. Application Not Responding

The dreaded "Not Responding" message can be alarming, especially if it happens frequently. Here's how I tackle this issue:

- **Wait and See**: Sometimes, an application becomes unresponsive because it's processing a large task. I wait a few minutes to see if the application recovers on its own, especially if I'm working with large files or complex operations.

- **End Task and Restart**: If the application remains unresponsive, I use Task Manager to end the task. I press Ctrl + Shift + Esc, find the application under the **Processes** tab, and select **End task**. After ending the task, I restart the application to see if the issue persists.
- **Check for Software Conflicts**: Similar to when an application crashes, conflicts with other software can cause it to stop responding. I try closing other applications and see if that resolves the issue. If the problem started after installing a new program, I consider uninstalling that program to see if it helps.
- **Repair or Reinstall the Application**: Some applications have a built-in repair option that can fix corrupted files. If that's available, I use it. If not, I uninstall and reinstall the application, ensuring I have the latest version.

5. Compatibility Issues

Compatibility issues arise when an application isn't fully supported on your version of Windows. Here's how I manage these situations:

- **Check for Compatibility Updates**: Some older applications may have updates or patches available that make them compatible with newer versions of Windows. I visit the official website to see if such updates are available.
- **Use Compatibility Mode**: If updates aren't available, I try running the application in compatibility mode. This involves right-clicking on the application's icon, going to **Properties > Compatibility**, and selecting an earlier version of Windows.
- **Virtual Machine or Emulator**: For legacy software that absolutely won't run on modern Windows versions, I consider using a virtual machine or emulator that can mimic an older operating system. This can be a bit more involved, but it's a reliable way to run older applications.

6. Licensing and Activation Issues

Occasionally, issues arise related to the licensing or activation of an application. This can prevent the software from functioning properly or restrict access to certain features.

- **Check License Status**: I verify that the application's license is still valid and hasn't expired. If it's a subscription-based service, I make sure my payment details are up to date and that the subscription hasn't lapsed.
- **Re-activate the Application**: Sometimes, re-activating the software can resolve licensing issues. I look for an option within the application to enter the license key again or contact the vendor's support team for assistance.
- **Reinstall the Application**: In cases where the licensing system seems corrupted or stuck, I uninstall and then reinstall the application. This often resets the activation process and resolves the issue.

Windows Store Apps

Windows Store apps, also known as Microsoft Store apps, have become an integral part of the Windows ecosystem, offering a wide range of software that's easy to install, update, and manage. However, like any software, these apps can sometimes present problems, ranging from installation issues to performance glitches. Here's how I typically troubleshoot and resolve common issues with Windows Store apps.

1. Installation Issues

One of the most common problems users encounter with Windows Store apps is difficulty installing them. Whether the app won't download, gets stuck during installation, or fails with an error code, these steps can help resolve the issue.

- **Check Internet Connection**: The first thing I do is ensure my internet connection is stable. A weak or intermittent connection can cause issues with downloading and installing apps from the Windows Store.
- **Clear the Microsoft Store Cache**: Sometimes, the Store's cache can become corrupted, leading to installation problems. I clear the cache by opening the **Run** dialogue (`Win + R`), typing `wsreset.exe`, and pressing Enter. This resets the Store without affecting installed apps.
- **Check Storage Space**: If there's insufficient storage space on my PC, the app may fail to install. I check my disk space by going to **Settings > System > Storage** and freeing up space if needed.
- **Update Windows**: Outdated versions of Windows can cause compatibility issues with new apps. I ensure my system is up to date by going to **Settings > Update & Security > Windows Update** and checking for updates.
- **Run Windows Store Troubleshooter**: Windows includes a built-in troubleshooter for the Microsoft Store. I go to **Settings > Update & Security > Troubleshoot**, find the **Windows Store Apps** option, and run the troubleshooter to detect and fix any issues.

2. App Crashes or Freezes

Another common issue with Windows Store apps is that they may crash or freeze during use. Here's how I handle these problems:

- **Update the App**: Developers frequently release updates to fix bugs and improve performance. I open the Microsoft Store, go to the **Library**, and check for updates for the app in question.
- **Reinstall the App**: If updating doesn't work, I uninstall the app and then reinstall it. I do this by right-clicking on the app in the Start menu, selecting **Uninstall**, and then reinstalling it from the Microsoft Store.

- **Check App Permissions**: Some apps require specific permissions to function properly. I go to **Settings > Privacy**, find the relevant permissions (like Camera, Microphone, or Background apps), and ensure the app has the necessary permissions enabled.
- **Run the App Troubleshooter**: Similar to installation issues, I can use the Windows Store Apps troubleshooter to address crashes and freezes. This tool can identify underlying problems and suggest fixes.

3. App Not Opening

Occasionally, an app may refuse to open at all. This can happen for a variety of reasons, but the following steps usually help get things working again:

- **Restart the PC**: Sometimes, a simple restart can resolve issues with apps that won't open. I restart my PC and try launching the app again.
- **Reset the App**: If the app still won't open, I reset it to its default state. I go to **Settings > Apps > Apps & features**, find the app in question, click **Advanced options**, and select **Reset**. This will delete the app's data but usually resolves the issue.
- **Sign Out and Back Into the Microsoft Account**: Issues with the Microsoft account associated with the Store can prevent apps from opening. I sign out of my account by going to **Settings > Accounts** and then sign back in to see if that resolves the problem.
- **Re-register Microsoft Store Apps**: If the app still won't open, I re-register all Microsoft Store apps using PowerShell. I open PowerShell as an administrator and run the following command:

```
powershell
```

- ```
  Get-AppXPackage   |   Foreach  {Add-AppxPackage  -
  DisableDevelopmentMode                 -Register
  "$($_.InstallLocation)\AppXManifest.xml"}
  ```
- This command re-registers all installed Store apps, which can fix issues with apps not opening.

4. Slow Performance

If a Windows Store app is running slowly or lagging, there are a few ways I approach the problem:

- **Close Background Apps**: Running too many apps simultaneously can strain system resources. I use Task Manager to close unnecessary background apps and free up resources for the Store app.
- **Disable Background Processes**: Some apps continue running in the background even when not in use, which can affect performance. I go to **Settings > Privacy > Background apps** and turn off background activity for apps I don't need.
- **Adjust Visual Effects**: High visual effects settings can slow down apps, especially on older or less powerful PCs. I go to **Settings > System > About** and select **Advanced system settings**. Under **Performance**, I choose **Adjust for best performance** to reduce visual effects.
- **Check for App-Specific Settings**: Some apps have settings that allow you to adjust performance-related options. I explore the app's settings menu to see if there are options to reduce resource usage or improve performance.

5. Update or License Issues

Sometimes, an app may fail to update, or there may be issues related to licensing, especially with paid apps.

- **Verify Payment Information**: If I'm having trouble updating or accessing paid content, I check that my payment
  ```

information in the Microsoft Store is up to date. I go to the **Microsoft Store > Account > Payment options** to verify or update my payment details.

- **Restore Purchases**: For apps that have in-app purchases or subscriptions, I ensure that my purchases are restored. This option is usually found within the app's settings or account menu.
- **Contact Support**: If an app fails to update or there are licensing issues that I can't resolve, I contact Microsoft Support or the app's developer for assistance. They can provide specific guidance or reset licenses if necessary.

6. Syncing Issues with Microsoft Account

Some apps require syncing with a Microsoft account, and issues here can affect app functionality.

- **Check Sync Settings**: I make sure that my sync settings are correctly configured by going to **Settings > Accounts > Sync your settings**. I ensure that the sync is turned on and that the correct account is being used.
- **Verify Account Credentials**: If there are issues with syncing, I check that my Microsoft account credentials are correct and that there are no issues with the account itself, such as two-factor authentication blocking access.
- **Re-Sync the App**: Some apps have a manual sync option. I look for this in the app's settings and try re-syncing to see if it resolves the issue.

Identifying Hardware Failures

When your Windows PC starts behaving erratically—crashing unexpectedly, refusing to boot, or running much slower than usual— it's natural to suspect software issues first. However, these symptoms can also point to underlying hardware failures. Identifying hardware problems early can save you a lot of frustration and potentially prevent further damage. Here's how I approach diagnosing hardware failures on a Windows PC.

1. Understanding Common Hardware Failure Symptoms

Before diving into diagnostics, it's essential to recognize the signs that point to possible hardware failures. These symptoms often include:

- **Frequent Crashes or Blue Screens of Death (BSODs)**: While software issues can cause crashes, frequent BSODs often indicate hardware problems, such as failing RAM or a malfunctioning hard drive.
- **Unusual Noises**: Grinding, clicking, or beeping sounds can signal hard drive failure, fan issues, or power supply problems.
- **System Overheating**: Overheating can lead to sudden shutdowns and is often a sign of failing cooling systems, such as the CPU fan or thermal paste degradation.
- **Sluggish Performance**: A sudden drop in performance, especially if accompanied by freezing or lagging, might point to failing hardware like the hard drive or power supply.
- **Failure to Boot**: If the system won't boot or stalls during startup, this could indicate issues with the motherboard, power supply, or storage device.

2. Diagnosing Specific Hardware Components

Once you've identified potential hardware failure symptoms, the next step is to diagnose which component is at fault. Here's how I go about it:

a. Hard Drive Issues

- **Run CHKDSK**: One of the first tools I use to check the health of a hard drive is CHKDSK. I open Command Prompt as an administrator and type `chkdsk /f` to scan for and fix file system errors. If I suspect bad sectors, I use `chkdsk /r`.
- **Listen for Unusual Noises**: Clicking or grinding noises from the hard drive are clear indicators of mechanical failure. In this case, I back up my data immediately and consider replacing the drive.
- **Use SMART Tools**: SMART (Self-Monitoring, Analysis, and Reporting Technology) is built into most modern drives and can provide detailed health reports. I use tools like CrystalDiskInfo to check the SMART status for signs of impending failure.

b. Memory (RAM) Issues

- **Run Windows Memory Diagnostic**: If I suspect faulty RAM, I start by running the Windows Memory Diagnostic tool. I search for "Windows Memory Diagnostic" in the Start menu, run the tool, and choose to restart the computer to check for memory errors.
- **Test with MemTest86**: For a more thorough test, I use MemTest86, a free tool that runs from a bootable USB. It performs a series of tests on the RAM to detect any errors that could be causing system instability.

c. Power Supply (PSU) Issues

- **Check PSU with a Multimeter**: If the PC is experiencing power issues—such as random shutdowns, reboots, or no power at all—I might test the power supply with a multimeter to check the voltage output on different rails.
- **Use a PSU Tester**: Alternatively, I can use a dedicated PSU tester, which is simpler and safer for those unfamiliar with multimeters. This device will quickly indicate whether the PSU is delivering the correct voltages.
- **Look for Physical Signs**: Burn marks, frayed cables, or a strong electrical smell can also indicate a failing power supply.

d. CPU and Cooling Issues

- **Monitor CPU Temperatures**: Overheating CPUs can cause crashes and slowdowns. I use tools like HWMonitor or Core Temp to check CPU temperatures. If they're consistently high, I may need to clean the CPU fan, reapply the thermal paste, or check for proper airflow inside the case.
- **Check for Physical Damage**: I also inspect the CPU socket and the motherboard for any signs of physical damage, such as bent pins or burned areas.

e. Graphics Card (GPU) Issues

- **Check for Artifacts**: Artifacts—strange visual glitches or distortions—on the screen can indicate GPU failure. If I see these during gaming or video playback, it's a strong sign of a problem.
- **Test with FurMark**: FurMark is a GPU stress testing tool that can help reveal whether the GPU is functioning correctly under load. If the system crashes or displays artefacts during the test, the GPU might be failing.
- **Monitor GPU Temperatures**: Overheating can also affect the GPU's performance. I use tools like MSI Afterburner to

monitor temperatures and ensure the GPU isn't running too hot.

f. Motherboard Issues

- **Check for Beep Codes**: If the PC won't boot, I listen for beep codes during startup. These codes can provide valuable clues about what's wrong. Each motherboard manufacturer has its own beep code system, so I refer to the manual or the manufacturer's website for details.
- **Inspect for Physical Damage**: I also look for signs of physical damage on the motherboard, such as bulging capacitors, burn marks, or loose connections. These can indicate electrical issues or component failure.

3. Using Diagnostic Tools

In addition to manual checks, I often use various diagnostic tools to help identify hardware failures:

- **BIOS/UEFI Diagnostics**: Many motherboards include built-in diagnostic tools accessible through the BIOS/UEFI. These tools can perform basic tests on hardware components like the CPU, RAM, and storage devices.
- **Third-Party Diagnostic Software**: Tools like HWiNFO, AIDA64, and Sandra provide detailed information about system hardware and can help pinpoint issues.
- **Stress Tests**: Running stress tests on components like the CPU (using Prime95) or GPU (using FurMark) can reveal weaknesses or failures when the hardware is under heavy load.

4. Repair or Replace?

Once I've identified the faulty component, the next decision is whether to repair or replace it:

- **Hard Drive**: If a hard drive is failing, I typically recommend replacing it rather than attempting repairs, especially if it's making noise or has a lot of bad sectors.
- **RAM**: Faulty RAM is usually replaced, as it's relatively inexpensive and repair isn't practical.
- **Power Supply**: A failing power supply should be replaced immediately to avoid damaging other components.
- **Motherboard or CPU**: If the motherboard or CPU is the issue, replacement can be more complex and costly. Depending on the age of the system, it might be worth considering a full upgrade instead of replacing just one component.
- **GPU**: If the GPU is failing and the system is used for gaming or graphic-intensive tasks, replacing the GPU is often necessary. However, for basic tasks, using integrated graphics might be a temporary workaround.

Display and Sound Issues

Dealing with display and sound issues on a Windows PC can be frustrating, especially when they disrupt your work or entertainment. Whether it's a blank screen, flickering display, no sound, or distorted audio, these problems often have straightforward solutions. Here's how I typically troubleshoot and resolve common display and sound issues.

1. Display Issues

a. No Display or Blank Screen

When you turn on your PC and the screen remains blank, it's often a sign of a problem with the display connection, the graphics card, or the monitor itself. Here's how I approach the situation:

- **Check Connections**: The first thing I do is ensure that all cables (HDMI, DisplayPort, VGA) are securely connected to both the monitor and the PC. If possible, I try a different cable or port to rule out a faulty connection.

- **Test with Another Monitor**: To determine if the monitor is the issue, I connect the PC to another monitor or TV. If the display works on the second screen, the original monitor may need repair or replacement.
- **Reset Display Settings**: Sometimes, incorrect display settings can cause issues. I restart the PC in Safe Mode (which uses basic display settings) and adjust the display resolution. I do this by pressing Shift + Restart, selecting **Troubleshoot > Advanced options > Startup Settings**, and then pressing 4 or F4 to start in Safe Mode. Once in Safe Mode, I right-click on the desktop, select **Display settings**, and choose a lower resolution to see if that restores the display.
- **Check for BIOS/UEFI Beep Codes**: If the screen remains blank from the moment you turn on the PC, it could be a graphics card issue. I listen for any beep codes during startup, as these can indicate hardware failures. If the PC has a dedicated graphics card, I might try switching to the integrated graphics to see if the issue is with the GPU.

b. Flickering or Distorted Display

A flickering or distorted display can be caused by driver issues, a faulty monitor, or even interference from nearby electronic devices. Here's how I handle it:

- **Update Graphics Drivers**: Outdated or corrupted graphics drivers are a common cause of display problems. I update the drivers by going to **Device Manager > Display adapters**, right-clicking the graphics card, and selecting **Update driver**. I choose **Search automatically for drivers** to let Windows find and install the latest version.
- **Check Refresh Rate**: An incorrect refresh rate can cause flickering. I right-click on the desktop, select **Display settings > Advanced display settings**, and ensure the refresh rate is

set to a value supported by the monitor (usually 60Hz or 75Hz).

- **Disable Hardware Acceleration**: Sometimes, hardware acceleration in specific applications (like browsers) can cause display issues. I go into the settings of the problematic application and disable hardware acceleration to see if it resolves the issue.
- **Test with a Different Monitor**: To rule out a faulty monitor, I connect the PC to a different display. If the flickering persists on another monitor, the issue might be with the graphics card or cable.

c. Resolution Issues

If the screen resolution is incorrect or not displaying as expected, I take these steps:

- **Adjust Display Resolution**: I right-click on the desktop and select **Display settings**. From there, I adjust the resolution to match the monitor's native resolution.
- **Update or Reinstall Graphics Drivers**: If the correct resolution isn't available, it could be due to outdated or corrupted graphics drivers. I update or reinstall the drivers as mentioned earlier.
- **Check for Scaling Issues**: If text or icons appear blurry or too large, I check the scaling settings. I go to **Display settings > Scale and Layout** and adjust the scaling percentage. Sometimes, setting it to 100% or a custom value can fix the issue.

2. Sound Issues

a. No Sound

When there's no sound coming from the speakers or headphones, it's usually an issue with the audio settings, drivers, or connections. Here's how I troubleshoot it:

- **Check Connections**: I start by ensuring the speakers or headphones are properly connected to the PC. If using external speakers, I check the power and volume settings as well.
- **Set Default Playback Device**: Sometimes, the wrong playback device is selected. I right-click on the sound icon in the system tray, select **Sounds**, and go to the **Playback** tab. From there, I set the correct device as the default by right-clicking it and selecting **Set as Default Device**.
- **Run Audio Troubleshooter**: Windows includes a built-in troubleshooter for audio issues. I right-click the sound icon in the system tray, select **Troubleshoot sound problems**, and follow the on-screen instructions to diagnose and fix the issue.
- **Update or Reinstall Audio Drivers**: If there's still no sound, I check the audio drivers. I open **Device Manager > Sound, video and game controllers**, right-click on the audio device, and select **Update driver**. If updating doesn't help, I might uninstall the driver and then restart the PC to let Windows reinstall it automatically.

b. Distorted or Crackling Sound

Distorted or crackling sounds can be caused by driver issues, interference, or hardware problems. Here's how I approach the issue:

- **Update Audio Drivers**: Outdated or corrupted drivers can cause audio distortions. I update the drivers as mentioned above.
- **Disable Audio Enhancements**: Audio enhancements can sometimes cause issues with sound quality. I go to **Playback devices**, right-click the default device, select **Properties**, and navigate to the **Enhancements** tab. I then check the box for **Disable all enhancements**.

- **Check for Interference**: Wireless devices, such as Wi-Fi routers or Bluetooth devices, can interfere with audio equipment. I try moving these devices away from the PC or switching to a wired connection to see if the issue persists.
- **Change Audio Format**: If the sound quality is poor, I might change the audio format. I go to **Playback devices**, right-click on the default device, select **Properties**, and navigate to the **Advanced** tab. From there, I experiment with different sample rates and bit depths to find the best setting.

c. Audio Device Not Detected

If Windows isn't detecting your audio device, it could be due to driver issues, a faulty port, or incorrect settings. Here's what I do:

- **Check Connections**: I make sure the device is properly connected to the correct port. If it's a USB device, I try plugging it into a different USB port.
- **Enable Disabled Devices**: Sometimes, the audio device might be disabled in the sound settings. I right-click the sound icon in the system tray, select **Sounds**, and go to the **Playback** tab. I right-click in the blank area and choose **Show Disabled Devices**, then enable any that are disabled.
- **Reinstall Audio Drivers**: If the device still isn't detected, I uninstall and reinstall the audio drivers as described earlier. I might also check for any available BIOS/UEFI updates, as these can sometimes fix hardware detection issues.

Dealing with Malware and Viruses

Malware and viruses are serious threats that can compromise the security of your Windows PC, damage files, and affect performance. Dealing with these threats effectively involves a combination of preventive measures and reactive troubleshooting. Here's how I handle malware and viruses on a Windows PC.

1. Understanding Malware and Viruses

Before diving into solutions, it's essential to understand what malware and viruses are:

- **Malware**: A broad term for malicious software designed to harm or exploit systems, including viruses, worms, trojans, ransomware, spyware, and adware.
- **Viruses**: A type of malware that attaches itself to legitimate files or programs and spreads to other files or systems, often causing damage or stealing information.

2. Preventive Measures

Preventing malware and viruses is crucial in maintaining a secure system. Here's how I stay protected:

a. Install and Update Antivirus Software

- **Choose Reliable Antivirus Software**: I use well-known antivirus programs such as Bitdefender, Norton, or Windows Defender, which provide real-time protection against threats.
- **Keep Software Updated**: I ensure that the antivirus software is always up to date with the latest virus definitions and security patches. This helps protect against new threats.

b. Enable Windows Defender

- **Activate Windows Defender**: Windows Defender is built into Windows and offers robust protection. I ensure it's enabled by going to **Settings > Privacy & Security > Windows Security** and checking that it's turned on.
- **Run Regular Scans**: I schedule regular scans using Windows Defender to catch any potential threats. I go to **Windows Security > Virus & threat protection > Quick scan** or **Full scan**.

c. Keep Windows and Software Updated

- **Enable Automatic Updates**: I make sure that Windows Update is set to automatically download and install updates. This includes security patches that protect against known vulnerabilities.
- **Update All Software**: I regularly update other software, including browsers and plugins, as outdated software can be a target for malware.

d. Practice Safe Browsing and Email Habits

- **Avoid Suspicious Links and Attachments**: I don't click on unknown or suspicious links in emails or websites. I also avoid downloading attachments from untrusted sources.
- **Use Strong Passwords**: I use strong, unique passwords for all accounts and consider using a password manager to keep track of them.
- **Enable Two-Factor Authentication (2FA)**: For added security, I enable 2FA on accounts that support it.

3. Detecting Malware and Viruses

If I suspect that my system is infected, I use the following methods to detect malware and viruses:

a. Run a Full System Scan

- **Use Antivirus Software**: I start by running a full system scan with my installed antivirus software to detect and remove any malware. This can be done from within the software's interface.

b. Use Malware Removal Tools

- **Windows Defender Offline Scan**: For more severe infections, I use Windows Defender Offline, which performs a scan before Windows starts. I access it through **Settings > Privacy & Security > Windows Security > Virus & threat protection > Scan options** and select **Windows Defender Offline scan**.
- **Third-Party Malware Removal Tools**: I might use tools like Malwarebytes or AdwCleaner, which specialize in detecting and removing malware that traditional antivirus software might miss.

c. Check for Unusual Behavior

- **Monitor System Performance**: Sluggish performance, unexpected pop-ups, or unfamiliar programs running in the background can be signs of malware. I use Task Manager (Ctrl + Shift + Esc) to monitor processes and identify any suspicious activity.
- **Review Installed Programs**: I go to **Control Panel > Programs and Features** to check for any unfamiliar or recently installed programs that could be malware.

4. Removing Malware and Viruses

Once detected, I follow these steps to remove malware and viruses:

a. Quarantine or Remove Threats

- **Use Antivirus Software**: If my antivirus software finds threats, I follow its recommendations to quarantine or remove the malware. Quarantining isolates the malware, preventing it from causing harm while allowing me to review and remove it if necessary.

b. Manually Remove Malware

- **Boot into Safe Mode**: I often boot into Safe Mode to prevent malware from running during the removal process. I do this by restarting the PC and pressing `F8` or `Shift + F8` during startup to access the Advanced Boot Options menu, then selecting Safe Mode.
- **Remove Malicious Files and Programs**: In Safe Mode, I manually delete suspicious files and uninstall unwanted programs. I use tools like Autoruns to identify and remove malicious startup entries.

c. Restore the System to a Previous State

- **Use System Restore**: If malware removal doesn't resolve the issue, I use System Restore to revert the system to a previous, clean state. I access this by searching for **System Restore** in the Start menu and following the prompts to restore the system to a date before the infection occurred.

5. After Removal

Once the malware is removed, I take these additional steps:

a. Change Passwords

- **Update Passwords**: I change passwords for all accounts, especially if there's a possibility that credentials may have been compromised.

b. Back-Up Data

- **Create Backups**: I back up important data to an external drive or cloud storage to prevent data loss in case of future infections.

c. Monitor System for Recurrence

- **Watch for Symptoms**: I keep an eye on the system for any signs of malware recurrence and run regular scans to ensure that the system remains clean.

Data Privacy and Protection

In today's digital age, protecting your personal and sensitive data is crucial. Data breaches, unauthorized access, and identity theft are growing concerns, and safeguarding your information requires a proactive approach. Here's how I manage data privacy and protection on my Windows PC.

1. Understanding Data Privacy and Protection

Data Privacy: Refers to the control and security of personal information, ensuring it is collected, stored, and used responsibly.

Data Protection: Involves measures to secure data from unauthorized access, breaches, and loss, ensuring its integrity and confidentiality.

2. Implementing Privacy Settings

a. Configure Windows Privacy Settings

- **Review Privacy Settings**: I access the privacy settings by going to **Settings > Privacy**. Here, I review and adjust settings related to location, camera, microphone, and other permissions to ensure only necessary apps have access.

- **Turn Off Ad Tracking**: I disable ad tracking to prevent personalized ads by going to **Settings > Privacy > General** and turning off **Let apps use advertising ID**.

b. Manage App Permissions

- **Check App Permissions**: I review and manage app permissions by going to **Settings > Privacy** and selecting each category (e.g., Camera, Microphone). I ensure that only trusted apps have access to sensitive information.
- **Remove Unnecessary Apps**: I uninstall apps that I no longer use or trust to reduce potential privacy risks.

3. Securing Personal Data

a. Use Strong Passwords and Authentication

- **Create Strong Passwords**: I use unique and complex passwords for each account. I often use a combination of uppercase letters, lowercase letters, numbers, and symbols.
- **Enable Two-Factor Authentication (2FA)**: I activate 2FA for my online accounts wherever possible. This adds an extra layer of security by requiring a second form of verification in addition to the password.

b. Encrypt Sensitive Data

- **Enable BitLocker**: For protecting data on my hard drive, I use BitLocker, a built-in Windows encryption tool. I activate it by going to **Control Panel > System and Security > BitLocker Drive Encryption** and following the prompts to encrypt the drive.

- **Use Encryption for Files**: For sensitive files, I use file encryption tools like VeraCrypt to ensure data is protected when transferred or stored.

4. Backing Up Data

a. Use Built-in Backup Tools

- **Set Up Windows Backup**: I use Windows Backup to create regular backups of my files. I access this through **Settings > Update & Security > Backup** and set up **File History** to back up my files to an external drive or network location.

b. Use Cloud Storage

- **Backup to Cloud Services**: I use cloud storage services such as OneDrive, Google Drive, or Dropbox to back up important files. This provides an additional layer of security and access from multiple devices.

5. Protecting Against Unauthorized Access

a. Use a Password Manager

- **Manage Passwords Securely**: I use a reputable password manager to store and generate strong passwords. This helps prevent password reuse and ensures my passwords are secure.

b. Lock Your PC

- **Use Lock Screen Features**: I configure my PC to require a password or PIN when waking from sleep or after a period of inactivity. This can be set up by going to **Settings > Accounts > Sign-in options** and choosing a suitable method.

6. Protecting Online Activities

a. Use a VPN

- **Encrypt Internet Traffic**: I use a Virtual Private Network (VPN) to encrypt my internet traffic, which protects my data from eavesdropping on public Wi-Fi networks. I choose a reliable VPN service and connect to it when accessing sensitive information online.

b. Be Cautious with Public Wi-Fi

- **Avoid Sensitive Transactions**: I avoid accessing sensitive accounts or performing financial transactions over public Wi-Fi. If necessary, I use my VPN to add a layer of security.

7. Staying Informed and Vigilant

a. Keep Software Updated

- **Regular Updates**: I ensure that Windows and all installed software are regularly updated to protect against vulnerabilities and security flaws. This includes applying security patches and updates promptly.

b. Monitor for Data Breaches

- **Check Breach Alerts**: I use services like Have I Been Pwned to monitor if my email addresses have been involved in data breaches. If so, I change the affected passwords immediately.

c. Educate Yourself

- **Stay Informed**: I keep up with the latest news on data privacy and cybersecurity best practices to stay informed about new threats and protective measures.

Handling File Corruption and Loss

File corruption and loss are frustrating issues that can disrupt your work and cause data loss. Whether it's due to a software malfunction, hardware failure, or accidental deletion, knowing how to handle these problems can help you recover your data and minimize damage. Here's how I approach file corruption and loss:

1. Understanding File Corruption and Loss

File Corruption: This occurs when a file becomes damaged or unreadable due to issues like software crashes, improper shutdowns, or malware.

File Loss: Refers to situations where files are accidentally deleted, lost due to hardware failure, or become inaccessible due to various reasons.

2. Preventing File Corruption and Loss

a. Regular Backups

- **Create Regular Backups**: I regularly back up important files using Windows Backup or third-party backup solutions. I schedule automatic backups to an external drive or cloud storage to ensure my data is protected.
- **Use Multiple Backup Locations**: I keep backups in multiple locations (e.g., local drive, external drive, cloud) to reduce the risk of losing all copies in case of hardware failure or other issues.

b. Use Reliable Software

- **Keep Software Updated**: I ensure that my operating system and applications are up to date to prevent bugs and vulnerabilities that could lead to file corruption.
- **Use Trusted Applications**: I avoid using unreliable or unverified software that could potentially cause file damage.

3. Dealing with File Corruption

a. Restore from Backup

- **Recover from Backup**: If a file becomes corrupted, I first check if I have a recent backup of the file. I restore the file from the backup to replace the corrupted version.

b. Use File Repair Tools

- **Use Built-In Windows Tools**: Windows includes some tools for file repair. For example, I can use **CHKDSK** to check and repair file system errors. I run it by opening Command Prompt as an administrator and typing `chkdsk /f` followed by the drive letter.
- **Use Third-Party Repair Tools**: If the built-in tools don't work, I use third-party file repair tools like DiskInternals or Stellar Phoenix, which can repair corrupted files and recover lost data.

c. Check for System Issues

- **Run System File Checker (SFC)**: If file corruption is part of a broader system issue, I run the System File Checker tool to scan and repair system files. I do this by opening Command Prompt as an administrator and typing `sfc /scannow`.
- **Use DISM Tool**: If SFC doesn't resolve the issue, I use the Deployment Imaging Service and Management Tool (DISM) to fix Windows corruption errors. I open Command Prompt as

an administrator and type `DISM /Online /Cleanup-Image /RestoreHealth`.

4. Handling File Loss

a. Check Recycle Bin

- **Recover from Recycle Bin**: If a file is accidentally deleted, I first check the Recycle Bin. If the file is there, I can easily restore it by right-clicking the file and selecting **Restore**.

b. Use File Recovery Software

- **Employ Recovery Tools**: If the file is not in the Recycle Bin, I use file recovery software like Recuva, EaseUS Data Recovery Wizard, or Disk Drill. These tools can scan my drive for deleted files and attempt to recover them.
- **Follow Recovery Instructions**: I follow the software's instructions to scan the drive and recover the lost files. It's best to recover files to a different drive to avoid overwriting any potential recoverable data.

c. Restore Previous Versions

- **Use Previous Versions**: If System Protection is enabled, Windows may have saved previous versions of files. I can access this feature by right-clicking the file or folder, selecting **Properties**, and going to the **Previous Versions** tab to restore an earlier version.

5. Preventing Future Issues

a. Regular Maintenance

- **Perform Disk Cleanups**: I regularly run Disk Cleanup to remove temporary files and system junk that could contribute

to file system problems. I access this by searching for **Disk Cleanup** in the Start menu and following the prompts.
- **Check for Disk Errors**: I periodically check my drives for errors using the **CHKDSK** tool mentioned earlier to prevent file system corruption.

b. Use Reliable Hardware

- **Maintain Hardware**: I ensure that my hard drives and SSDs are in good condition. I monitor their health using tools like CrystalDiskInfo or the manufacturer's diagnostics software.
- **Replace Failing Hardware**: If hardware issues are detected, I replace failing drives or components promptly to prevent

Managing Disk Partitions

Disk partitions are essential for organizing data, optimizing performance, and managing storage on a Windows PC. Properly managing partitions can help in data organization, system backups, and efficient use of disk space. Here's how I approach disk partition management:

1. Understanding Disk Partitions

Disk Partitioning: The process of dividing a physical disk into multiple logical sections, each of which functions as an independent unit. Partitions can be used to separate system files, applications, and personal data.

2. Viewing and Managing Partitions

a. Access Disk Management

- **Open Disk Management**: I access Disk Management by right-clicking on the Start menu and selecting **Disk**

Management, or by typing `diskmgmt.msc` in the Run dialog (Windows + R). This tool provides an overview of all disks and partitions.

b. View Partition Information

- **Check Disk Layout**: In Disk Management, I review the layout of my partitions, including the size, file system, and partition type. This helps me understand how my disk space is allocated and identify any issues.

3. Creating and Deleting Partitions

a. Create a New Partition

- **Shrink Existing Partition**: To create a new partition, I first need unallocated space. If none is available, I shrink an existing partition. In Disk Management, I right-click on the partition I want to shrink and select **Shrink Volume**. I specify the amount of space to shrink and create unallocated space.
- **Create New Partition**: Next, I right-click on the unallocated space and select **New Simple Volume**. I follow the New Simple Volume Wizard to specify the size, assign a drive letter, and format the partition with the desired file system (usually NTFS).

b. Delete a Partition

- **Delete a Partition**: To remove a partition, I right-click on it in Disk Management and select **Delete Volume**. I confirm the deletion, which will erase all data on the partition and convert it to unallocated space.

4. Resizing Partitions

a. Extend a Partition

- **Use Unallocated Space**: To extend a partition, it must have adjacent unallocated space. I right-click on the partition I want to extend and select **Extend Volume**. I specify the amount of space to add from the unallocated space and complete the process.

b. Resize with Third-Party Tools

- **Use Partition Software**: For more complex resizing needs, such as moving partitions or resizing partitions without adjacent unallocated space, I use third-party tools like EaseUS Partition Master or MiniTool Partition Wizard. These tools offer more flexibility and options for managing partitions.

5. Optimizing Disk Performance

a. Check for Fragmentation

- **Run Defragmentation**: For traditional HDDs, I periodically defragment the disk to optimize performance. I access this by searching for **Defragment and Optimize Drives** in the Start menu and selecting the appropriate drive for defragmentation.

b. Use Solid State Drives (SSDs)

- **Avoid Defragmentation**: For SSDs, defragmentation is not necessary and can reduce the lifespan of the drive. Instead, I ensure that TRIM is enabled, which helps maintain SSD performance by managing unused blocks. I check TRIM status through Command Prompt with the command `fsutil behaviour query DisableDeleteNotify`.

6. Handling Disk Partition Issues

a. Fix Partition Errors

- **Run CHKDSK**: To check for and fix partition errors, I use the Check Disk utility. I open Command Prompt as an administrator and run `chkdsk [drive letter]: /f` to scan and repair errors on the specified drive.

b. Recover Lost Partitions

- **Use Recovery Tools**: If a partition is lost or not showing up, I use recovery tools like TestDisk or EaseUS Partition Recovery. These tools can scan the disk for lost partitions and attempt to recover them.

7. Best Practices for Partition Management

a. Plan Partition Layout

- **Organize Data**: I plan my partition layout based on my needs, such as separating system files, applications, and personal data. This helps with data organization and system backups.

b. Regular Backups

- **Backup Data**: Before making changes to disk partitions, I ensure that my data is backed up. This protects against data loss in case of mistakes or issues during partition management.

c. Monitor Disk Health

- **Check Disk Health**: I use tools like CrystalDiskInfo to monitor the health of my disks. Regular checks can help identify potential issues before they lead to data loss or hardware failure.

Common Update Problems

Windows updates are essential for maintaining system security, stability, and performance. However, issues can sometimes arise during the update process, leading to incomplete installations or system errors. Here's how I address common update problems on a Windows PC:

1. Update Installation Failures

a. Check for Error Codes

- **View Error Codes**: When an update fails, Windows usually provides an error code. I note this code, as it helps diagnose the issue. I check for details on the error code by searching for it in the Windows Update Troubleshooter or online.

b. Run the Windows Update Troubleshooter

- **Access Troubleshooter**: I run the built-in Windows Update Troubleshooter by going to **Settings > Update & Security > Troubleshoot > Additional troubleshooters** and selecting **Windows Update**. This tool can identify and fix common issues.

c. Manually Download and Install Updates

- **Use Microsoft Update Catalog**: If automatic updates fail, I manually download the update from the Microsoft Update Catalog. I search for the update by its KB number and install it manually.

2. Update Stuck at Certain Percentage

a. Restart the Update Process

- **Restart PC**: If an update is stuck, I restart my PC to see if it resolves the issue. Sometimes, a simple reboot can prompt the update to continue.

b. Clear Windows Update Cache

- **Delete Temporary Files**: I clear the Windows Update cache by stopping the Windows Update service, deleting the contents of the `SoftwareDistribution` folder, and restarting the service. I open Command Prompt as an administrator and run:

```
arduino
```
- net stop wuauserv
- net stop cryptSvc
- net stop bits
- net stop msiserver
- ren   C:\Windows\SoftwareDistribution SoftwareDistribution.old
- ren C:\Windows\System32\catroot2 Catroot2.old
- net start wuauserv
- net start cryptSvc
- net start bits
- net start msiserver
-

3. Update Reverts or Rolls Back

a. Check for System Issues

- **Run System File Checker (SFC)**: I run SFC to check for and repair corrupted system files. In Command Prompt as an administrator, I use the command `sfc /scannow`.
- **Use DISM Tool**: If SFC doesn't resolve the issue, I run the Deployment Imaging Service and Management Tool (DISM)

with the command `DISM /Online /Cleanup-Image /RestoreHealth`.

b. Update Device Drivers

- **Check Drivers**: Sometimes, outdated or incompatible drivers can cause issues with updates. I check for driver updates in **Device Manager** and update them as needed.

4. Update Errors Related to Disk Space

a. Free Up Disk Space

- **Clear Space**: I free up disk space by using **Disk Cleanup** to remove temporary files, system cache, and other unnecessary files. I access Disk Cleanup by searching for it in the Start menu.

b. Move or Delete Files

- **Relocate Large Files**: I move large files or applications to another drive or external storage if disk space is critically low.

5. Update Issues After Restart

a. Perform a Clean Boot

- **Boot in Safe Mode**: I perform a clean boot to eliminate potential conflicts with third-party software. I do this by typing `msconfig` in the Run dialogue, going to the **Services** tab, checking **Hide all Microsoft services**, and then clicking **Disable all**. I restart my PC and attempt the update again.

b. Check for Software Conflicts

- **Review Installed Software**: I review recently installed or updated software that might conflict with Windows Update. I uninstall or update conflicting software as needed.

6. Network-Related Update Problems

a. Reset Network Settings

- **Flush DNS and Reset TCP/IP**: I reset network settings by flushing the DNS cache and resetting TCP/IP settings. I run the following commands in Command Prompt as an administrator:

```perl
perl
```
- `ipconfig /flushdns`
- `netsh int ip reset`
-

b. Check Internet Connection

- **Verify Connection**: I ensure that my internet connection is stable and working properly, as a weak or intermittent connection can cause update problems.

7. Windows Update Service Issues

a. Restart Windows Update Service

- **Restart Service**: I restart the Windows Update service to resolve issues with update installations. I do this by going to **Services** (type `services.msc` in the Run dialogue), finding **Windows Update**, and clicking **Restart**.

b. Re-register Windows Update Components

- **Re-register Components**: I re-register Windows Update components if problems persist. I do this by running the following commands in Command Prompt as an administrator:

```bash
bash
```
- `regsvr32.exe /u wuaueng.dll`
- `regsvr32.exe wuaueng.dll`
-

8. Final Steps

a. Check for Additional Updates

- **Install Other Updates**: Sometimes, installing other pending updates can resolve issues with the problematic update. I check for additional updates in **Settings > Update & Security > Windows Update**.

b. Seek Microsoft Support

- **Contact Support**: If I'm still unable to resolve the issue, I consider contacting Microsoft Support for further assistance. They can provide specialized help based on the specific error codes and symptoms.

Upgrading Windows OS

Upgrading your Windows operating system can enhance performance, security, and access to new features. Here's how I approach upgrading my Windows OS to ensure a smooth transition and minimal disruption.

1. Preparation for Upgrade

a. Check System Requirements

- **Review Compatibility**: Before upgrading, I check the system requirements for the new Windows version to ensure my hardware is compatible. I review the official Microsoft website for these requirements.

b. Backup Important Data

- **Create Backups**: I back up important files and documents to an external drive or cloud storage. This ensures that my data is protected in case anything goes wrong during the upgrade.

c. Update Current System

- **Install Updates**: I make sure that my current Windows version is up to date by installing the latest updates. This can help prevent compatibility issues during the upgrade process.

2. Choosing an Upgrade Method

a. Upgrade Through Windows Update

- **Check for Updates**: I check for the upgrade option in **Settings > Update & Security > Windows Update**. If the new Windows version is available for upgrade, I can start the process here.
- **Follow Prompts**: I follow the on-screen instructions to download and install the upgrade. This method is typically straightforward and ensures that the upgrade process is handled automatically.

b. Use the Windows Installation Assistant

- **Download Installation Assistant**: If the upgrade isn't available through Windows Update, I download the Windows Installation Assistant from the Microsoft website or the corresponding page for my Windows version.

- **Run the Assistant**: I run the Installation Assistant and follow the prompts to download and install the new Windows version.

c. Perform a Clean Installation

- **Create Installation Media**: For a fresh start, I create installation media using the Media Creation Tool. I download the tool from the Microsoft website or the corresponding page for my Windows version and use it to create a bootable USB drive or DVD.
- **Perform Clean Install**: I boot from the installation media and follow the prompts for a clean installation. This method involves formatting the drive and installing the new Windows version from scratch, so I ensure that all important data is backed up before proceeding.

3. During the Upgrade Process

a. Follow On-Screen Instructions

- **Complete Installation**: I follow the on-screen instructions provided by the upgrade tool or installation assistant. This includes choosing preferences, setting up a user account, and configuring initial settings.

b. Ensure Stable Power Supply

- **Keep PC Powered**: To avoid interruptions, I ensure that my PC is connected to a reliable power source during the upgrade process, especially if I'm using a laptop.

4. Post-Upgrade Steps

a. Check for Updates

- **Install Additional Updates**: After upgrading, I check for any additional updates by going to **Settings > Update & Security > Windows Update**. Installing these updates ensures that my system has the latest patches and improvements.

b. Restore Data and Reinstall Applications

- **Restore Backed-Up Data**: I restore my files from the backup I created before the upgrade.
- **Reinstall Applications**: I reinstall any applications or drivers that were not carried over during the upgrade. I check for the latest versions compatible with the new Windows version.

c. Verify System Performance

- **Check System Health**: I review the system's performance to ensure everything is running smoothly. I check for any issues with hardware or software compatibility and address them as needed.

d. Update Drivers

- **Update Device Drivers**: I visit the manufacturer's website or use Windows Update to ensure that all device drivers are updated and compatible with the new Windows version.

5. Troubleshooting Post-Upgrade Issues

a. Address Compatibility Issues

- **Check for Issues**: If I encounter compatibility issues with applications or hardware, I check the manufacturer's website for updates or fixes. I may also use compatibility mode to run older applications.

b. Resolve Performance Problems

- **Optimize Performance**: If I experience performance issues, I perform routine maintenance tasks such as disk cleanup, defragmentation (for HDDs), and checking for malware.

c. Seek Support

- **Contact Microsoft Support**: If I encounter persistent issues that I cannot resolve, I contact Microsoft Support for assistance.

Chapter 10: Advanced Troubleshooting Tools and Techniques

Using System Diagnostics Tools

System diagnostics tools are essential for troubleshooting and maintaining the health of your Windows PC. They help identify hardware and software issues, monitor system performance, and provide insights into potential problems. Here's how I use these tools effectively:

1. Windows Built-in Diagnostics Tools

a. Task Manager

- **Monitor Performance**: I use Task Manager to view real-time performance data, including CPU, memory, disk, and network usage. I open it by pressing `Ctrl + Shift + Esc` or right-clicking the taskbar and selecting **Task Manager**.
- **Identify Resource Hogs**: In the **Processes** tab, I identify applications and processes consuming high resources. This helps in pinpointing issues related to system slowdowns or crashes.

b. Performance Monitor

- **Access Performance Monitor**: I access Performance Monitor by typing `perfmon` in the Run dialogue (Windows + R). This tool provides detailed system performance data.
- **Create Custom Reports**: I use Performance Monitor to set up custom data collector sets and create performance reports, which can help diagnose specific performance issues.

c. Reliability Monitor

- **View System History**: I access Reliability Monitor by typing `reliability` in the Start menu search. It provides a timeline of system events and errors.
- **Check for Issues**: I review the **Reliability Monitor** to identify and address recurring issues or critical errors reported by the system.

d. Event Viewer

- **Open Event Viewer**: I open Event Viewer by typing `eventvwr` in the Run dialog. This tool logs detailed information about system events and errors.
- **Review Logs**: I review the **Windows Logs** and **Application and System Logs** to identify error messages or warnings that can help diagnose problems.

e. System File Checker (SFC)

- **Run SFC Scan**: I use the System File Checker to scan and repair corrupted system files. I open Command Prompt as an administrator and run `sfc /scannow`.

f. Deployment Imaging Service and Management Tool (DISM)

- **Repair System Image**: If SFC doesn't resolve the issue, I use DISM to repair the system image. In Command Prompt as an administrator, I run `DISM /Online /Cleanup-Image /RestoreHealth`.

2. Advanced Diagnostics Tools

a. Windows Memory Diagnostic

- **Run Memory Test**: I use Windows Memory Diagnostic to check for memory (RAM) issues. I access it by typing `mdsched` in the Run dialogue and follow the prompts to restart and test memory.

b. Check Disk Utility (CHKDSK)

- **Scan and Repair Disks**: I use CHKDSK to check for and repair disk errors. I open Command Prompt as an administrator and run `chkdsk [drive letter]: /f` to scan and fix errors on the specified drive.

3. Third-Party Diagnostic Tools

a. Hardware Monitoring Tools

- **Use Tools like HWMonitor or Speccy**: I use third-party tools such as HWMonitor or Speccy to monitor hardware health, including temperatures, voltages, and fan speeds.

b. Disk Health Tools

- **Check with CrystalDiskInfo**: I use CrystalDiskInfo to check the health status of my hard drives and SSDs, monitoring attributes like temperature, wear level, and error rates.

c. System Stress Testing Tools

- **Perform Stress Tests**: Tools like Prime95 or AIDA64 help stress test my CPU and memory to ensure stability under load. I use these tests to diagnose potential issues with hardware performance.

4. Interpreting Diagnostics Results

a. Analyzing Data

- **Understand Results**: I carefully review the results from diagnostic tools to identify patterns or recurring issues. For example, high temperatures in hardware monitoring tools might indicate cooling problems.

b. Troubleshooting Based on Results

- **Address Issues**: Based on the diagnostic results, I take appropriate actions. For instance, if CHKDSK reports bad sectors, I might consider replacing the affected drive.

5. Regular Maintenance

a. Schedule Regular Checks

- **Perform Routine Diagnostics**: I schedule regular use of these diagnostic tools to proactively monitor system health and catch issues early.

b. Keep Tools Updated

- **Update Software**: I ensure that all diagnostic tools, both built-in and third-party, are kept up to date to benefit from the latest features and fixes.

Remote Troubleshooting

Remote troubleshooting allows me to diagnose and resolve issues on a computer without being physically present. This is especially useful for providing technical support to others or managing multiple systems. Here's how I approach remote troubleshooting effectively:

1. Setting Up Remote Access

a. Enable Remote Desktop

- **Windows Pro and Above**: If I need to access a Windows PC remotely, I ensure that Remote Desktop is enabled on the target machine. I go to **Settings > System > Remote Desktop**, toggle the **Enable Remote Desktop** switch, and make a note of the PC's name.
- **Firewall Settings**: I check that the firewall allows Remote Desktop connections. This is usually configured automatically when enabling Remote Desktop but can be verified in **Control Panel > System and Security > Windows Defender Firewall > Allow an app or feature through Windows Defender Firewall**.

b. Use Remote Assistance

- **Invite Someone**: I use Windows Remote Assistance for one-time remote help. I open it by searching for **Remote Assistance** in the Start menu and choose **Invite someone you trust to help you**. I can then send an invitation via email or save it to a file.

c. Third-Party Remote Access Tools

- **Choose a Tool**: I use third-party tools like TeamViewer, AnyDesk, or Chrome Remote Desktop if Remote Desktop is not an option. These tools often provide more features and ease of use.
- **Install and Configure**: I install the chosen tool on both the host and remote computers, configure access permissions, and ensure that both machines are connected to the internet.

2. Establishing a Remote Connection

a. Connect via Remote Desktop

- **Use Remote Desktop Connection**: I open **Remote Desktop Connection** by typing `mstsc` in the Run dialog. I enter the

PC's name or IP address and click **Connect**. I then provide the required credentials to access the remote machine.

b. Connect via Third-Party Tools

- **Start a Session**: I open the third-party remote access tool on both devices. I enter the access credentials or session code provided by the remote tool to establish a connection.

3. Conducting Remote Troubleshooting

a. Communicate Effectively

- **Stay in Touch**: I keep clear and constant communication with the person on the other end to guide them through the process and ensure that they are following the instructions correctly.

b. Assess the Issue

- **Understand the Problem**: I start by asking detailed questions about the issue to get a clear understanding. I then use diagnostic tools or perform tests remotely to identify the problem.

c. Perform Troubleshooting Steps

- **Apply Fixes**: I perform troubleshooting steps as if I were at the computer. This may include checking system settings, running diagnostic tools, or modifying configurations.
- **Monitor Progress**: I keep track of any changes or results and adjust the troubleshooting steps based on the feedback and outcomes.

4. Security Considerations

a. Use Secure Connections

- **Encrypt Connections**: I ensure that remote access tools use encrypted connections to protect data transmitted over the internet.
- **Update Software**: I keep remote access and security software up to date to protect against vulnerabilities.

b. Manage Permissions

- **Limit Access**: I only grant necessary permissions for the task at hand and ensure that remote access is terminated once the troubleshooting session is complete.
- **Monitor Access**: I use tools that allow me to monitor and control remote sessions to prevent unauthorized access.

5. Ending the Remote Session

a. Disconnect Securely

- **Terminate Connection**: Once troubleshooting is complete, I close the remote session securely by using the disconnect feature in the remote access tool.

b. Review and Document

- **Document Actions**: I document the steps taken and any changes made during the session for future reference or follow-up.
- **Review with User**: I review the outcomes with the user to ensure that the issue is resolved and address any additional questions they might have.

6. Follow-Up

a. Provide Support

- **Offer Additional Help**: I offer additional support if needed and provide instructions for any follow-up actions the user may need to take.

b. Schedule Check-Ins

- **Plan Future Check-Ins**: I schedule follow-up sessions if necessary to ensure that the issue remains resolved and to check for any new problems.

Command Line Troubleshooting

When dealing with issues on a Windows PC, the Command Line Interface (CLI) is one of the most powerful tools in my troubleshooting arsenal. It allows me to execute commands directly, bypassing the graphical user interface (GUI) to diagnose and resolve problems efficiently. Here's how I utilize command-line troubleshooting effectively:

1. Accessing the Command Line Interface

a. Command Prompt (CMD)

- **Open CMD**: I open Command Prompt by typing `cmd` in the Start menu search or by pressing `Windows + R`, typing `cmd`, and hitting Enter. For administrative tasks, I right-click on Command Prompt and select **Run as administrator**.

b. PowerShell

- **Open PowerShell**: PowerShell is a more advanced command-line tool. I open it by typing `powershell` in the Start menu search or by pressing `Windows + X` and selecting **Windows PowerShell**. To run it with elevated privileges, I select **Windows PowerShell (Admin)**.

c. Windows Terminal

- **Use Windows Terminal**: In newer versions of Windows, I prefer using Windows Terminal, which supports multiple tabs for CMD, PowerShell, and other shells. I access it from the Start menu or by typing `wt` in the Run dialog.

2. Basic Troubleshooting Commands

a. System Information

- **System Info**: To gather detailed information about the system, I use the `systeminfo` command. This provides a summary of the operating system, hardware, network, and more.

- `systeminfo`

- **Check for IP Configuration**: To view network configuration details, I use `ipconfig` to display IP addresses, subnet masks, and default gateways.

    - `ipconfig`
    -

b. Checking Disk and File System Health

- **Check Disk (CHKDSK)**: I use `chkdsk` to check for and repair file system errors on a drive. Running it with the `/f` flag fixes any issues found.

    ```bash
    bash
    ```
- `chkdsk C: /f`

- **Check Free Space**: To see the available and used space on all drives, I use the `dir` command.

```
bash
```
- `dir C:`
-

c. Repairing System Files

- **System File Checker (SFC)**: I use `sfc /scannow` to scan and repair corrupted system files. This is especially useful when system stability is compromised due to corrupted files.

  ```bash
  bash
  ```
- `sfc /scannow`

- **Deployment Imaging Service and Management Tool (DISM)**: If SFC doesn't resolve the issue, I use `DISM` to repair the system image. This command checks the health of the Windows image and repairs it if needed.

```mathematica
mathematica
```
- `DISM /Online /Cleanup-Image /RestoreHealth`
-

3. Networking Troubleshooting

a. Diagnosing Network Issues

- **Ping Command**: To test connectivity to another device, I use `ping` followed by the IP address or hostname. This command helps me determine if a network connection is working.

- `ping google.com`

- **Trace Route (TRACERT)**: If I need to trace the path that data takes to reach a particular server, I use `tracert`. This helps in diagnosing where the connection is breaking down.

- `tracert google.com`

- **Netstat**: To view active connections and listening ports, I use `netstat`. This helps in identifying open connections and potential security issues.

- `netstat -an`

- **Release and Renew IP Address**: If I'm dealing with IP address conflicts, I release and renew the IP address using `ipconfig /release` followed by `ipconfig /renew`.

```bash
```
- `ipconfig /release`
- `ipconfig /renew`
-

4. Advanced Command Line Tools

a. Managing Processes

- **Tasklist and Taskkill**: I use `tasklist` to display a list of running processes and `taskkill` to terminate any problematic processes.

  ```
  r
  ```
- `tasklist`
- `taskkill /IM processname.exe /F`
-

b. Managing Services

- **Net Start/Stop**: To manage services, I use `net start` to start a service and `net stop` to stop it. This is useful when troubleshooting service-related issues.

```
arduino
```
- `net start servicename`
- `net stop servicename`
-

c. Managing Disk Partitions

- **Diskpart**: I use `diskpart` for advanced disk management tasks like creating, deleting, and formatting partitions. It's a powerful tool, so I use it cautiously.

- `diskpart`

- **Listing Volumes**: To list all volumes on the system, I use `list volume` after launching `diskpart`.

  - `list volume`
  -

5. Troubleshooting Boot Issues

a. Bootrec

- **Repair Bootloader**: If the system fails to boot, I use `bootrec` with various options to repair the bootloader. For instance, `bootrec /fixmbr` fixes the Master Boot Record, while `bootrec /fixboot` writes a new boot sector.

```bash
```
- `bootrec /fixmbr`
```
bootrec /fixboot
```

- **Rebuild Boot Configuration Data (BCD)**: If the BCD is corrupted, I rebuild it using `bootrec /rebuildbcd`.

```bash
```

- `bootrec /rebuildbcd`
-

b. BCDedit

- **Edit Boot Configuration**: To manually edit the boot configuration, I use `bcdedit`. This command is powerful but should be used with caution to avoid rendering the system unbootable.

  ```bash
  bash
  ```
- `bcdedit /set {bootmgr} displaybootmenu yes`
-

6. Automating Troubleshooting with Scripts

a. Batch Files

- **Automate Tasks**: I create batch files (`.bat`) to automate repetitive troubleshooting tasks. For instance, I can automate a series of diagnostic checks and save time during the troubleshooting process.

b. PowerShell Scripts

- **Advanced Automation**: For more advanced automation, I use PowerShell scripts. These can automate complex tasks and integrate with various Windows components.

  ```vbnet
  vbnet
  ```
- `Get-Process | Where-Object { $_.CPU -gt 1000 }`

Maintenance and Best Practices

When it comes to maintaining a Windows PC, proactive care is just as important as reactive troubleshooting. By following preventive maintenance routines and adhering to best practices, I can significantly reduce the likelihood of encountering issues, extend the lifespan of the hardware, and ensure optimal performance. Here's how I approach preventive maintenance and the best practices I recommend:

1. Regular System Updates

a. Keep Windows Updated

- **Windows Update**: I ensure that Windows is always up to date by regularly checking for updates. I do this by going to **Settings > Update & Security > Windows Update** and clicking **Check for updates**. Keeping the system updated helps protect against vulnerabilities and improves system stability.
- **Driver Updates**: In addition to Windows updates, I make sure that all device drivers are up to date. Outdated drivers can cause hardware compatibility issues and degrade performance. I typically check for driver updates through **Device Manager** or the manufacturer's website.

b. Software Updates

- **Update Applications**: I regularly update all installed software, including web browsers, productivity tools, and security software. This helps protect against security vulnerabilities and ensures compatibility with other system components.

- **Automate Updates**: Where possible, I enable automatic updates for both the operating system and applications to ensure that I'm always using the latest versions.

2. Regular System Backups

a. Backup Data Regularly

- **Use Built-in Backup Tools**: I use Windows' built-in backup tools, like **File History** and **System Image Backup**, to regularly back up important files and create system restore points. This ensures that I can quickly recover from system failures, data corruption, or accidental deletions.
- **External Backup Solutions**: For added security, I use external hard drives or cloud storage solutions to back up critical data. This provides a fallback in case of hardware failures or major system issues.

b. Test Restore Procedures

- **Verify Backups**: I regularly test my backup and restore procedures to ensure that backups are complete and restorable. This helps avoid unpleasant surprises in the event of a real disaster.

3. Disk Maintenance

a. Disk Cleanup

- **Remove Unnecessary Files**: I use the **Disk Cleanup** tool to remove temporary files, system cache, and other unnecessary data that can accumulate over time. This helps free up disk space and improve system performance.

- `Cleanmgr`
-
- **Delete Browser Cache**: Regularly clearing browser cache and cookies helps improve browser performance and protects privacy.

b. Defragmentation

- **Defrag Hard Drives**: For traditional hard drives (HDDs), I run **Disk Defragmenter** to reorganize fragmented data and improve read/write speeds. SSDs typically do not need defragmentation, but Windows automatically optimizes them.

  ```mathematica
  defrag C:
  ```
-
- **Automate Defragmentation**: I schedule defragmentation to run automatically at regular intervals, typically weekly, to ensure that the drive remains optimized.

4. Security Practices

a. Use Reliable Security Software

- **Install Antivirus**: I ensure that reliable antivirus software is installed and kept up to date. This provides a first line of defence against malware, viruses, and other malicious threats.
- **Enable Firewall**: The Windows Firewall is crucial for preventing unauthorized access to the system. I always keep it enabled and configure it to block unnecessary connections.

b. Regular Scans

- **Schedule Regular Scans**: I schedule regular full-system antivirus scans to catch any threats that may have slipped through real-time protection. I also periodically scan for rootkits and other advanced threats using specialized tools.

c. Safe Browsing Practices

- **Avoid Suspicious Links**: I practice safe browsing by avoiding suspicious links, email attachments, and websites. Enabling browser security features, such as pop-up blockers and phishing filters, further enhances protection.
- **Use Strong Passwords**: I ensure that all accounts use strong, unique passwords, and I enable two-factor authentication (2FA) where possible. Password managers help in generating and storing secure passwords.

5. Hardware Maintenance

a. Keep Hardware Clean

- **Regular Cleaning**: I regularly clean the interior of the PC, removing dust from fans, vents, and other components. Dust buildup can cause overheating and reduce the efficiency of cooling systems.
- **Check Connections**: I ensure that all cables, RAM modules, and other internal components are securely connected. Loose connections can cause random shutdowns, data corruption, or boot failures.

b. Monitor Hardware Health

- **Temperature Monitoring**: I use hardware monitoring tools to keep an eye on temperatures, especially for the CPU and GPU. High temperatures can lead to thermal throttling and hardware damage, so I ensure that cooling solutions are adequate.
- **Check Hard Drive Health**: I periodically check the health of hard drives using tools like **CrystalDiskInfo**. Monitoring

S.M.A.R.T. data can give early warnings of potential drive failures, allowing me to back up data before a failure occurs.

6. Performance Optimization

a. Manage Startup Programs

- **Reduce Startup Impact**: I use Task Manager to manage startup programs, disabling unnecessary applications that slow down the boot process. This improves system startup times and overall responsiveness.

b. Resource Management

- **Monitor Resource Usage**: I regularly monitor system resource usage through Task Manager to identify and address resource-hogging applications that could slow down the system.
- **Optimize Power Settings**: I adjust power settings based on usage, balancing performance and energy consumption. For desktops, I usually opt for the **High-Performance** plan, while laptops might benefit from the **Balanced** or **Power Saver** plans.

7. User Account Management

a. Use Standard Accounts

- **Limit Admin Privileges**: For daily use, I operate under a standard user account instead of an administrator account. This minimizes the risk of accidentally installing malware or making system-altering changes.

b. Set Up Parental Controls

- **Control Access**: On family computers, I set up parental controls to restrict access to inappropriate content and limit the usage of certain applications. This helps maintain system integrity and protect younger users.

8. Documentation and Logging

a. Keep Logs

- **Document Changes**: I maintain a log of system changes, such as software installations, updates, and hardware modifications. This documentation helps in troubleshooting by providing a history of what might have led to a problem.

b. Use Event Viewer

- **Monitor Logs**: I regularly check the **Event Viewer** for any critical errors or warnings that could indicate underlying issues. Addressing these early can prevent larger problems down the road.